# A M HINE THEY'RE
# SEC ETLY BUILDING

By Andrew Westerside and Proto-type Theater

## CAST

| | |
|---|---|
| A | Rachel Baynton |
| B | Gillian Lees |

## CREATIVE TEAM

| | |
|---|---|
| **Writer & Director** | Andrew Westerside |
| **Digital Artist & Designer** | Adam York Gregory |
| **Composer & Original Sound Designer** | Paul J. Rogers |
| **Stage Manager** | Tom Marcinek |
| **Company Producer** | Gillian Lees |
| **Consultant Producer** | Matt Burman |

*A Machine they're Secretly Building* premiered at Lancaster Arts on Tuesday 2nd February 2016. It was commissioned by Lincoln Performing Arts Centre, Warwick Arts Centre and hÄb (Manchester). Supported by Tramway (Glasgow), Lancaster Arts at Lancaster University, The Britten-Pears Foundation and The National Lottery through Arts Council England.

The critical introduction to this text was written by Dr Aylwyn Walsh, School of Performance and Cultural Industries, University of Leeds (UK).

## ANDREW WESTERSIDE (WRITER & DIRECTOR)

Andrew Westerside (Wes) is a performer, writer, director, academic and co-artistic director of Proto-type Theater. As a performer he has toured nationally and internationally, most recently in *Whisper*, *Virtuoso* and *Third Person: Bonnie and Clyde*.

His writing and directing credits include: *The Calmer Future*, *An Interview with Dorian Gray*, *The Good, the God and the Guillotine* and *A Machine they're Secretly Building*. He co-wrote and directed BBC Radio Lincolnshire's *Leaving Home* project, which told the story of Lincolnshire's Beechey family and their losses during World War One. Also for the BBC, he has written and directed *The Forgotten Suffragette* and *Fallen* (with Conan Lawrence). In 2015 he co-wrote and directed *In Their Name*, commissioned for the opening ceremony of the International Bomber Command Memorial.

He studied at Dartington College of Arts and completed his PhD at Lancaster University. His academic work has been published in journals including *Performance Research* and *Theatre & Performance Design* and he is currently working with Michael Pinchbeck on *Staging Loss: Performance-as-Commemoration*, a forthcoming book.

## PROTO-TYPE THEATER

Proto-type are a company of multi-disciplinary artists led by Rachel Baynton, Gillian Lees, and Andrew Westerside.

Proto-type create original performance work that is diverse in scale, subject and medium. Recently, this has included touring theatre (*A Machine they're Secretly Building*), a two-week long theatrical experience using pervasive technologies (*Fortnight*), a multimedia concert-performance featuring a live laptop orchestra and animation (*The Good, the God and the Guillotine*) and a radio drama with the BBC (*The Forgotten Suffragette*).

The company has been making work and supporting young artists in the US, the Netherlands, Russia, China, Armenia, France, Zimbabwe and the UK since 1997. Critics have called their work 'an intriguing brush with altered reality' (New York Times), 'daring, experimental and theatrically engaging' (Theatremania) and 'enthralling' (Zambezi News).

@Proto_type
proto-type.org
#AMTSB

## RACHEL BAYNTON (DEVISOR / PERFORMER)

Rachel Baynton is a writer, performer, producer and dramaturg. As co-artistic director of Proto-type Theater, she has made and toured work nationally and internationally, including *A Machine they're Secretly Building*, pervasive technology piece *Fortnight*, and multimedia concert-performance *The Good, the God and the Guillotine*.

Rachel studied at Dartington College of Arts, and went on to create the site-specific *Bulliver Project* (with the support of the South Devon Railway), and international writing collaboration, *Finish This*. She has worked with the BBC on radio drama *The Forgotten Suffragette* and on *Fallen*, an operatic chamber piece, performed live to commemorate and coincide with the 100th anniversary of the Battle of the Somme.

She has directed youth theatre companies in venues and festivals around the country, toured large-scale outdoor performances to English Heritage sites, and managed the collections at Lancaster University's Institute of Contemporary Arts (LICA). She is currently associate lecturer in the School of Fine and Performing Arts at the University of Lincoln.

## GILLIAN LEES (DEVISOR / PERFORMER)

Gillian Lees is a Glasgow based contemporary performance practitioner, working in contemporary theatre, live art and durational performance contexts.

Co-artistic director of Proto-type Theater, Gillian has performed in a number of works throughout the UK and internationally (including *Whisper*, *Virtuoso*, *Third Person: Bonnie and Clyde*, *The Good, the God and the Guillotine*, *A Machine they're Secretly Building*, and BBC radio piece *The Last Suffragette*). She also directed large-scale pervasive technology piece Fortnight at major arts venues across the UK.

She studied Contemporary Theatre Practice at the Royal Scottish Academy of Music and Drama, is an associate artist of Third Angel (collaborating on works including *9 Billion Miles* from *Home* and *A Perfect Circle*), a member of The Strange Names Collective and a frequent collaborator with artists and performance makers across the UK.

Gillian has a collaborative live art practice with visual artist Adam York Gregory. They have exhibited their works (*A Working Hypothesis*, *Constants & Variables*, *Time/Distance*, *Present Tense*, *Full Stop*) at internationally renowned venues, galleries and festivals, including Tempting Failure (London), Buzzcut (Glasgow), The Storey (Lancaster), dfbrl8r (Chicago IL), Mobius (Boston MA), Rosekill (NY) and Tramway (Glasgow).

## ADAM YORK GREGORY (DIGITAL ARTIST & DESIGNER)

Adam York Gregory is a scientist, designer, typographer, animator, film maker and visual artist. His practice explores the synergies and contradictions between these disparate pursuits, frequently through collaboration.

He has recently been touring durational live art, internationally, in collaboration with Gillian Jane Lees.

## PAUL J. ROGERS (COMPOSER & ORIGINAL SOUND DESIGNER)

Paul J. Rogers is a sound sculptor, producer and composer, whose recently published work includes CD albums as The Sevens Collective on Beta-lactam Ring Records (USA) and Mecapop Label (France), Second-Handed Blues on ASC Records (UK), The Long Dead Sevens on Beta-lactam Ring Records (USA), The Imaginary Delta on Slam Productions (UK) and a collaboration with Philippe Petit on Vinyl 10" on Alrealon Musique (France).

He currently has a number of film soundtracks being performed internationally at major film festivals including Canada, Australia, USA and across Europe, including a set of animations with English cartoonist Steven Appleby. He has soundtracks recorded and performed with theatre and dance companies, including Proto-type Theater, Pigeon Theatre, Forecast Dance & PickleHerring Theatre.

Paul mixes traditional song-writing with an experimental approach to electro-acoustic composition and sound manipulations. His research practice often focuses on the extraneous noises and sound junk aesthetics from waste recordings, discarded objects and environmental field recordings.

### Thanks

All our thanks to the following great people for their help, time and generosity: Hannah Baynton, Alice Booth, Matt Burman, Leo Burtin, Tamsin Drury, Jamie Eastman, Laura Elliot, Gavin Fowler, John Franklin, Adam York Gregory, Fenia Kotsopoulou, Conan Lawrence, Anne Lees, Tom Marcinek, David McBride, Craig Morrow, Tim Nunn, Peter S. Petralia, Paul J. Rogers, Samantha Stockdale, Ally Walsh, Manny Westerside, Ray Westerside and Mark Wilde.

A MACHINE THEY'RE SECRETLY BUILDING

# A MACHINE THEY'RE SECRETLY BUILDING

Andrew Westerside and Proto-type Theater

OBERON BOOKS
LONDON

WWW.OBERONBOOKS.COM

First published in 2017 by Oberon Books Ltd
521 Caledonian Road, London N7 9RH
Tel: +44 (0) 20 7607 3637 / Fax: +44 (0) 20 7607 3629
e-mail: info@oberonbooks.com
www.oberonbooks.com

A catalogue record for this book is available from the British
Library.

PB ISBN: 9781786821119
E ISBN: 9781786821126

Cover image by Adam York Gregory

Printed, bound and converted by
CPI Group (UK) Ltd, Croydon, CR0 4YY.

Visit www.oberonbooks.com to read more about all our books
and to buy them. You will also find features, author interviews and
news of any author events, and you can sign up for e-newsletters
so that you're always first to hear about our new releases.

*Dedicated to those who stand up,
speak out, and blow the whistle…*

## Staging the Radical Potential of the Imagination
### A Critical Introduction to *A Machine they're Secretly Building*
**By Aylwyn Walsh**

*A Machine they're Secretly Building* is a bold and uncompromising performance text that stages a world both steeped in history's excuses and titillated by the fearful prospects of the future. This future is marked out by the paradoxes of consumers who do not always attend to the implications of everyday life in the technological age. Proto-type Theater's most recent production takes on the significant questions of state violence, surveillance and the neoliberal erosion of civil liberties.

Two performers straddle a divide: in some scenes playing at warmongering, data gathering and surveillance and in others confessing that they are complicit in the world where to be human is to have a data footprint. And where having a data footprint means that one is legible to the state – not merely as a consumer, but as a person whose movements, associations, and choices are captured and stored. The performance text offers this kind of surveillance as prefaced by the Cold War and explicitly demarcates how contemporary global economics and politics trickle down to shape, discipline and delimit our daily lives. This is an urgent creative intervention in the era of the so-called 'Snooper's Charter', passed by the United Kingdom's parliament in November 2016. This law requires web and phone companies to store people's web browsing history for twelve months. It also provides police access to private information and to journalists' records. This sets the stage for a range of invasions of privacy, storage of data and surveillance within legal paradigms. Henry Giroux terms this the internalisation of surveillance 'disimagination'. What we can learn from *A Machine they're Secretly Building* is that this crisis, this inability to imagine alternatives to the status quo, is what theatre and performance is so perfectly equipped to challenge.

## Aesthetics: Technology and the Homemade

The stage fragments and shatters those narrative devices that are afforded in well-made plays: chronologies, nation-states and personal choice are shown as contingent, interrelated, and with consequences beyond their containers. This offers opportunities for staging including engagement with technologies, and yet the work also proposes the use of a helium balloon, a few foil hats, and Pussy-Riot style pink balaclavas. Westerside juxtaposes technology (live feed, as well as projections of historical found footage collated *à la* Adam Curtis) and the materiality of the homemade or decidedly luddite. These and other stylistic features position the work as contemporary performance in which deliberate attention is drawn to the construction of stage business. This aesthetic, prevalent in work by Gob Squad, Forced Entertainment, and Tim Crouch draws attention to the construction of images on stage. Thematically, too, the performance works at positioning the spectator within the crisis and reflecting upon it. Not as the source of (or responsible for) war, but as complicit within its mechanisms. As agents, and yet, somehow, as still bound up in the narratives, conventions and aesthetics that constitute the crisis. Far from being stuck in a mode of pessimism, however, *A Machine they're Secretly Building* draws focus to the power of communal action.

One of the paradoxes raised by the performance relates to notions of permanence vs. transience. Westerside's script shows the implications of surveillance and mass data storage in bunkers in the Nevada desert: that while lives around the world are disposable, and bodies are placed at risk due to precarity and austerity, the billions of gigabytes of information generated by browsing histories and consumer choices are not disposable. They are stored, monetised and valued in service of capital ventures.

This performance stages the implications of 'disimagination', which is possible because individuals come to believe the spectacle that such storage is synonymous with safety and security. The central crisis in the work is not the drone strike or mass surveillance or any apparatus of war and dispossession.

The crisis is the performance-in-response from people who are silenced by being ill-informed or not convinced that action will achieve anything. The question that is ultimately raised in this work is of what performance might do; this relates to the possibility/ potential/ the not-yet, not-here of Jill Dolan's 'utopian performative' In the face of crisis, utopia is not a luxury for speculative fiction lovers; it becomes a pedagogic and performative imperative.

## Developing a Performative Pedagogy

The performance mode of two bodies shifting eras, genders and characters allows for a rapid, internet-age byte-sized consumption of facts of the genealogies of states using surveillance. The work draws on the compelling stylishness of war-time spies but by developing the scenario from what might have been acceptable during the Cold War to the excessive data mining of today through to a dystopian not-too distant future, surveillance becomes a force that is inevitable, and tied to safety and security. In the show, surveillance is explicitly tied to terrorism (thus nation) as well as consumerism (and thus capital). The scenographic construction of space includes a technical element as half the stage projects multimedia footage, incorporating the 1972 World Chess Championship between Bobby Fischer (USA) and Boris Spassky (USSR) as exemplifying key moments in the Cold War. Proto-type's staging then turns surveillance cameras on the audience to isolate suspicious audience behaviours, modelled on developments in automated threat detection (similar to the EU-led INDECT project).

What makes this a performative pedagogy is that the work is as much about educating audiences about the implications of the crisis of disimagination in a global sense as it is about evoking individual dis-ease. This works alongside philosopher Cornelius Castoriadis' notion that we need to be 'constituting critical thinkers who are capable of putting institutions into question so that democracy can be nourished and sustained' (1997: 5).

## Historicising the Crisis of Violence, Spectacle and State Surveillance

The aesthetic space shifts between the UK and the USA while demonstrating the links between state behaviours in the present and the inextricable connections to the past. In addition, the implications of whistle-blowers such as Edward Snowden, Chelsea Manning, Julian Assange and the leaking of the Panama Papers are demonstrably linked with how states identify and then contain and monitor threats to public safety. Westerside shows that the conflation of safety with capital is ultimately servicing the current global crisis – and we can see the spectacle of safety and security fuelling the reactions to refugees across Europe, for example. Part of what this historical element does in the work is to create space to develop a productive 'us' vs 'them' rhetoric; and to begin to trouble this distinction. By this I mean a distinction that is not constituted on otherness but between 'we, the people' and the state.

## Us vs. Them

In the show, while the two performers narrate most of the facts in role, there are several instances where they step out of the scene and are recorded on a live feed camera, wearing bright pink balaclavas. These scenes are confessional, and the 'terrorist/anarchist' assemblage is adopted with paradoxical proximity to the audience. In these scenes, instead of the glossiness of 'facts', or the aesthetic of a vintage documentary, the fuzzy immediateness of tech of the youtube/facebook generation positions us alongside the confessing people. These people admit they are afraid and insecure, unable to distinguish between the real threats and the mediated threats. This kind of characterisation of 'us' and 'them' runs through many examples of contemporary performance and art-forms responding to the global crisis: Citizens vs. Refugees; Law-makers vs. Lawbreakers; those who support the state vs. anarchists.

## Agit-prop: Insisting on the Implication of the 'you' as an Agent of Change

As Jill Dolan shows in her characterisation of theatre as a utopian space, the work explicitly positions audiences as capable of agency. In theatre, she says, 'politics lie in the desire to feel the potential of elsewhere. The politics lie in our willingness to attend or to create performance at all, to come together in real places – whether theatres or dance clubs – to explore in imaginary spaces the potential of the "not yet" and the "not here"' (Dolan, 2005: 20). In this production, it is quite clear that much of the force of the work comes from understanding mass surveillance of citizens by states as a crisis in the here and now. Yet, *A Machine they're Secretly Building* marks out the legacies and implications of terrorism and national security and positions individual, confused, consumer-citizens as deeply imbricated within these mechanisms of control, panopticism and policing. By doing so, the work moves beyond representation and promotes a utopian performative that is fundamentally about resistance. I would hope to resuscitate this theory as not merely a jolly sense of hopefulness but as a politically charged potential.

Westerside's script offers multiple modes of performance as critique. It proposes the need for a radical imagination to work against the state's systemic, expanding and stultifying storage. Instead, for audiences and those wanting to stage this work, there is the possibility of imagining anew.

## References

Castoriadis, C. (1997) 'Democracy as Procedure and Democracy as Regime', *Constellations* 4(1): pp.1 – 18.

Dolan, J. (2010) *Utopia in Performance: Finding Hope at the Theater.* Ann Arbor: University of Michigan Press.

Giroux, H. (2015) *The Violence of Organized Forgetting: Thinking beyond America's Disimagination Machine.* San Francisco: City Lights.

# Characters

Two performers, A and B.
Roles are not gender-specific.
In this version of the script, A and B are female.
Gendered pronouns may be altered accordingly.

A third letter, S, refers to text
appearing on a projection screen.

## Setting

The piece is set in the theatre it is being performed in.
It might also resemble a bunker, a hideout,
a press conference, an interview room,
a holding cell or a meeting.

## Time

Now.

*(Downstage-left, just off centre-line, a table with two chairs positioned behind. On the table: a desk microphone, two copies of the script, a carafe of water and two glasses, a retractable pointer, two small piles of A5 paper, and two pencils. To the immediate stage-left of table, a four-drawer filing cabinet, preferably time-worn, its drawers facing stage-right. Downstage-right, just off centre-line, a projection screen. All text marked 'S' appears here, as well as additional video material selected at the discretion of the director. Upstage-centre, a video camera and tripod facing stage-left. The camera should be visible between the table and the screen. A live feed sends the camera image to the projection screen.*

*A is sitting on the chair stage-left. B stands in front of the camera. They are both wearing pink balaclavas. The camera is focussed on B's face, which is positioned on the stage-right half of the frame. S text in this opening section appears in the other half of the frame.)*

**SOUND:** A high pitched tone, fluctuating. Like static, or interference, but cleaner. Like ringing in your ears.

**S:**   Dear friend,

**S:**   I do not want to live in a world where everything I do and say is recorded

**S:**   It frightens me. Keeps me awake at night.

**S:**   But I think that's the road we're on.

**S:**   I don't think anyone meant it to be this way

**S:**   I think it happened by accident

**S:**   My government, your government, wants us to trade away our privacy, our freedom, for safety

**S:**   You are, on average, caught on CCTV 70 times, every day.

**S:**   In the UK alone, there are somewhere between 4.2 and 5.9 million CCTV cameras.

**S:**   Watching

**S:**   Keeping you safe

**S:**   But your safety isn't free. Your freedom, isn't free.

**S:**   You have to open your arms, your lives, to systems of surveillance so pervasive and invasive that slowly, without noticing, they change you.

**S:**   The way you act

**S:**   The way you think

**S:**   You become compliant

**S:**   You have **nothing to hide**

**S:**   Even if you're doing nothing wrong, you're being watched, and recorded

**S:**   …just in case.

**S:**   I don't want to trade privacy for security

**S:**   I don't want to live in a technological police state

**S:**   I don't want to spend my whole life believing there's monsters under the bed

**S:**   But I don't think it was supposed to be this way

**S:**   I think it happened by accident, slowly, without anyone really stopping to notice.

**S:**   And now I'm worried that we've almost gone too far

**S:**   That soon, we won't be able to turn the machine off

**S:**   And it'll be like this

**S:**   Forever.

**S:**   I can't in good conscience allow the U.S. government to destroy privacy, internet freedom and basic liberties for people around the world with this massive surveillance machine they're secretly building
                                             – Edward Snowden

**S:**   A MACHINE THEY'RE SECRETLY BUILDING

*(B moves from the camera to the vacant chair. Once sat, A and B remove their balaclavas and place them on the back of their chairs. They straighten their scripts.)*

**SOUND:** END – previous. START – office sounds, pre-digital. Hubbub, typewriters.

**A:**    The beginning
**B:**    The beginning
**A:**    London
**B:**    England
**A:**    1943
**B:**    Sirens

**SOUND:** START – air raid sirens, wireless broadcasts, signal interference

**A:**    Blackouts, Buzz Bombs.
**B:**    Early spring. It's raining.
**A:**    An office, in the city, its location unknown. Dark wood, dim lights. Suits, bowler hats, umbrellas.
**B:**    An agreement
**A:**    Called BRUSA. B-R-U-S-A
**B:**    The beginning of a relationship
**A:**    Full of promise
**B:**    Like this one, tonight
**A:**    Between us
**B:**    Between us.
**A:**    An agreement, called BRUSA. A contract. Between:
**B:**    Great Britain
**A:**    And
**B:**    The United States of America
**A:**    An agreement
**B:**    To share Signals Intelligence
**A:**    SIG-INT
**B:**    Information
**A:**    That will keep people safe
**B:**    That will end the war
**A:**    End the tears
**B:**    End the rain

**A:**   That will bring people home

**B:**   Home

**A:**   Alive.

**B:**   Information

**A:**   Intelligence

**B:**   Shipping routes

**A:**   Flight paths

**B:**   Troop movements

**A:**   Coded messages, transcribed by hand

**B:**   And delivered, by motorcycle despatch riders

**A:**   Or telegraph

**B:**   Or radio.

**A:**   They send locations

**B:**   Dates

**A:**   Times

**B:**   Names

**A:**   Anything that might tip the scales in their favour

**B:**   An advantage

**A:**   An edge

**B:**   And then

*(Pause.)*

**SOUND:** END – previous. START – 1940's big band music.

**A:**   1946

**B:**   After the rain

**A:**   Early spring. March

**B:**   An office, in the city. Again, location unknown.

**A:**   A ten-page document, marked 'top secret, to be kept under lock and key, never to be removed from the office'

**B:**   An agreement

**A:**   To *keep* spying

**B:**   To keep snooping

**A:**   To know

**B:**   To be one step ahead

**A:**   To make sure it doesn't happen again

*(They each sign a piece of paper, and exchange them.)*

**B:**     Two copies

        *(They sign the exchanged papers.)*

**B:**     *(Cont.)* Two signatures

        *(They exchange papers again.)*

**B:**     *(Cont.)* And a handshake

        *(They perform a handshake, as one might after signing a treaty or accord.)*

**A:**     The papers are sealed inside locked boxes, and taken away to top secret rooms for top secret secrets

**B:**     To keep you safe
**A:**     Don't worry, they said: trust us
**B:**     We'll keep you safe
**A:**     It's reasonable. It makes sense
**B:**     No more rain.
**A:**     Please
**B:**     No more rain
**A:**     So they build a machine
**B:**     A secret machine
**A:**     To keep you safe
**B:**     From them
**A:**     The others
**B:**     The ones like you
**A:**     But not you
**B:**     We'll keep you safe
**A:**     Trust us
**B:**     And the machine grows
**A:**     Gets stronger
**B:**     More capable
**A:**     And then

        *(Pause.)*

**SOUND:** END – Previous. START – Lou Reed, *Satellite of Love.*

**B:**    The Cold War.
**A:**    Korea
**B:**    Vietnam
**A:**    Guatamala
**B:**    Jakarta
**A:**    Cuba
**B:**    Iran. The Space Race
**A:**    1964. A new relationship: FIVE EYES.
**B:**    Great Britain. Government Communications
         Headquarters. GCHQ
**A:**    The United States. National Security Agency. NSA
**B:**    Australia
**A:**    New Zealand
**B:**    And Canada
**A:**    A new programme: ECHELON.
**B:**    A listening network, made of satellites

*(A opens the bottom drawer of the filing cabinet. Inside is a white helium-filled balloon, with a small light inside, tied to clear thread. It floats upwards, coming to rest high above the playing space. A and B lean back in their chairs, to look at it.)*

**A:**    Floating, in orbit
**B:**    Listening
**A:**    Watching
**B:**    Remembering
**A:**    Up there
**B:**    In the cold
**A:**    Off the books
**B:**    Out of sight

*(A sits forward.)*

**A:**    It doesn't exist

*(B sits forward.)*

**B:**    It doesn't exist
**A:**    If anyone asks
**B:**    It doesn't exist.
**A:**    They use radio.

**SOUND:** END – Previous. START – *The Lincolnshire Poacher (Numbers station version.)*

**A:**   *(Cont.)* Shortwave

**B:**   Unlicensed

**A:**   Untraceable

**B:**   Deniable

**A:**   They install intercept stations:

**B:**   In Munich. Codename: GARLICK

**A:**   Menwith Hill, Yorkshire. Codename: MOONPENNY

**B:**   Japan

**A:**   LADYLOVE

**B:**   Washington

**A:**   JACKNIFE

**B:**   Puerto Rico

**A:**   CORALINE

> *(During the following line, A reaches in to the bottom drawer of the filing cabinet and removes a pad of edible paper. A writes lists of five-digit numbers.)*

**B:**   Your recipient knows that at certain times on certain nights you will transmit, normally in five digit code groups. They are given a one-time pad, or OTP, of which only one other copy exists.

> *(A tears the front page out of the pad, and hands it to B.)*

**B:**   *(Cont.)* Yours.

> *(During the following line, B writes on the torn out sheet, as if deciphering the numbers.)*

**A:**   The pages of a one-time pad consist of different, random, five-digit groups of numbers that are used to encipher messages with the aid of a matrix, or number grid, that can be read much like the coordinates of a road map. Listen.

**SOUND:** END – previous. START – A numbers station broadcast, in English.

*(B stops writing, and listens. Then, with urgency:)*

**B:**     I don't know what I'm supposed to be doing. Repeat
         last message.

**A:**     Silence

**B:**     Hello? This is Munich. You're breaking up. I don't
         know what I'm doing. The pad, it's… Hello? Hello?

**A:**     Silence

**B:**     Shit!

*(They return to a calmer tone. During the following, B destroys
the torn out page. If the paper is edible, it can torn in to strips
and eaten. The eating can occur during the following line.
A returns the pad to the drawer, smoothly lowers the balloon,
and closes the drawer.)*

**B:**     Each page of the OTP is destroyed after use. Since
         only one other copy exists, the code is unbreakable.
         The recipient uses their copy of the one-time pad to
         decipher the message. The pad is on edible paper.
         Once they decipher the message, they tear the pages
         out, burn them, flush them down the toilet, or eat them
         – however they've been instructed.

**SOUND:** END – previous. START – A high pitched tone,
         mixed with static.

**A:**     And then they wait. For the rain.

**B:**     With cloud overhead. East looking West

**A:**     West looking East

**B:**     Stalemate

**A:**     Press the button

*(A reaches towards the desk microphone. Their hand is halted
by B.)*

**B:**     Don't

**A:**     Press the button

*(Again, A reaches towards the microphone and is halted.)*

**B:**     Don't.

**A:**     Waiting

**B:**     To fire

**A:**     To fight

**B:**     To explode

**A:**     Waiting.

*(Pause.)*

**B:**     Find them

**A:**     The Red Ones

**B:**     Neighbours

**A:**     Friends

**B:**     Colleagues

**A:**     Find them

**B:**     They're waiting

**A:**     Waiting

*(Pause.)*

**B:**     For a release

**A:**     For destruction

**B:**     But they can't fight. It's too close. Too close to call.

**A:**     So they play a game

**SOUND:** END – previous. START – The Rolling Stones, *Paint it Black.*

**B:**     A beautiful game

**A:**     1972. Reykjavik.

*(A stands.)*

**A:**     *(Cont.)* The match of the century

*(A opens the second drawer of the filing cabinet. From it they remove two small desk flags – one USA, one USSR – a bottle of vodka, and two shot glasses. A places the items on to the table. B arranges them.)*

**B:**     Bobby Fischer, the United States

**A:**     Versus

**B:**     Boris Spassky, the Soviet Union

**A:**    The world, shrunk to the size of a chess board.

*(A takes the retractable pointer from the table and moves to the stage-right edge of the projection screen. Through the following section of text, the screen and pointer should be used to show a representation of the chess moves as played in the 1972 World Championship final.)*

**B:**    Every move a tightrope act
**A:**    Deliberated over
**B:**    Every piece a weapon
**A:**    The perfect game
**B:**    The perfect metaphor
**A:**    The world watched
**B:**    And held its breath.
**B:**    Fischer, pawn to C4.
**A:**    Spassky, pawn to E6.
**B:**    Every possible mistake already on the board
**A:**    Sharp suits. Martinis. Sepia tones.
**B:**    Nixon. Brezhnev. Kissinger. Watergate. The propaganda. The back-channeling. It all, comes down, to this.
**A:**    To keep you safe.
**B:**    Aston Martins. Private Jets. James Bond stuff. Fischer, Pawn to E3. It's not a game, Boris. It's not a game.
**A:**    Fischer, Rook to F2. Spassky, Queen to E8
**B:**    Fischer, Rook to F3. Spassky, Queen to D8
**A:**    Fischer smells blood. It's almost over.
**B:**    Fischer, Bishop to D3. Spassky, Queen to E8
**A:**    He can't get out.

**SOUND:** *Paint it Black* distorts, stutters, is overwritten by a whistling tone and signal interference.

**B:**    Fischer, Queen to E4. Spassky, Knight to F6
**A:**    Fischer, Rook captures F6. Spassky, Pawn on B file captures F6.
**B:**    I've got him. I've got him.
**A:**    Fischer. Rook captures F6. Spassky, King to G8
**B:**    The King. Aim for the King.
**A:**    Fischer. Bishop to C4. Spassky, King to H8

**B:** Fischer. Queen to F4. Spassky Retires.

**A:** Spassky, retires.

**B:** It's over.

**A:** And the dust settles…

**SOUND:** END – previous. START – high pitched tone from the beginning.

*(A returns to the table, but remains standing. As A moves, B pours two shots of vodka.)*

**B:** Did we win?

**A:** I don't know. I think so…

*(They each pick up a shot of vodka. They toast.)*

**A:** Для нашей дружбы! (say: Za Na-shu Drooz-bu.)

**B:** Для нашей дружбы! (say: Za Na-shu Drooz-bu.)

**A:** But the *world* changed

*(A takes the vodka bottle and glasses, and places them on top of the filing cabinet.)*

**B:** The game changed

**A:** And the charm… disappeared.

*(B passes the flags to A, who puts them in the open second drawer.)*

**B:** The risk too high, and the reward too low. The pawns stopped lining up in nice, neat, rows.

**A:** Something big was on the horizon

**B:** Something new

*(A removes a 1970's style telephone from the second drawer.)*

**A:** A new piece of the machine

*(A moves upstage, and faces the camera.)*

**B:** Harvard University, 1975. One Hundred and Fifty-Seven Kilometres East of Hartford, Connecticut. A Lecture. Combinatorics.

**A:**     Albeuquerque, New Mexico. Three Thousand Five Hundred and Eight Kilometres West of Harvard. A bar. Oklahoma Joe's. Known as Okies.

**SOUND:** END – previous. START – The Bee Gees, *Jive Talkin'.*

*(A holds the receiver to their ear. A dances, as if bobbing to the music in a noisy bar.)*

**B:**     Bill where are you? I haven't seen you all semester.
**A:**     I'm in New Mexico. I don't think I'm coming back Steve
**B:**     What?
**A:**     I'm setting up a company
**B:**     Now? Bill that doesn't make any sense!
**A:**     It does. I have to do it now – look – I don't want to miss my chance. I've spoken to my parents, they're cool about it. Me and Paul, we're setting up an office in Albuquerque. We're calling it 'Micro'-'Soft'. Like, Micro Software. Come down, you'd love it here Steve!

**B:**     Bill, I hope you know what you're doing. This home computers thing… I don't know… I'm not sure it's got legs… Y'know, I don't think that name's great.

**A:**     Steve! The name's *brilliant!* What do you want me to do, name it after a piece of fruit?! I promise you, Steve, it's all going to work out – it's going to be incredible.

*(A returns to the table, and places the phone in the open drawer, then closes it. A sits.)*

**SOUND:** END – previous. START – high pitched tone.

**B:**     1978. A new programme.
**A:**     Codename: BLARNEY
**B:**     Phone call intercepts
**A:**     Faxes
**B:**     International mail
**A:**     Only, it was getting harder to know who the enemy was, if they even existed at all
**B:**     Keep looking

**A:** They exist

**B:** They exist

**A:** If anyone asks

**B:** They exist

**A:** Find them

**B:** Neighbours

**A:** Friends

**B:** Colleagues

**A:** Find them

**B:** But they *couldn't* find them

**A:** Until the fuse was already lit

**B:** Until it was too late.

**A:** 1986, the West Bank

**B:** 1988, Lockerbie

**A:** 1992, Yemen

**B:** 1993, New York

**A:** 1994, Hebron

**B:** 1998, Dar es Salaam, Tanzania, Nairobi

**A:** On, and on, and on, and on.

**B:** Panic.

**A:** The sky, lighting up, like fireworks

**B:** A match

**A:** A fizz

**B:** A bang

**A:** Followed, always, by an awful silence

**SOUND:** END – previous.

*(Pause.)*

**B:** And then

**A:** The tipping point.

**B:** 1991

**A:** The Conseil Européen pour la Recherche Nucléaire

**B:** Better known, as CERN

**A:** Eight Kilometres North-West of Geneva. In, of course, the cafeteria.

**SOUND:** START – an analogue clock, ticking.

*(A and B slump in their chairs, exhausted.)*

**B:**    Tim, we've got to give it a name. We've got to call it
         *something.*

**A:**    What about the World-Wide Web?

         *(B sits up, excited. They both return to a straight sitting position.)*

**B:**    A blink

**A:**    Silence…

**B:**    A flicker

**A:**    Silence…

**B:**    And an explosion

**SOUND:** END – previous. START – sounds of the computer
         age. Bleeps, bings, recycle bins, and the Windows
         95 boot sound. A cacophony of noise sourced from
         electronic devices.

**A:**    An explosion. Mobile phones

**B:**    ARPANET

**A:**    NPL

**B:**    Networks

**A:**    Servers

**B:**    Chat Rooms

**A:**    IRC

**B:**    File-Sharing

**A:**    Electronic Mail

**B:**    Webcams

**A:**    Webinars

**B:**    Spam

**A:**    Shopping

**B:**    Don't go out. We'll bring stuff to you.

**A:**    Stay in

**B:**    Stay online

**A:**    Stay safe

**B:**    Passwords

**A:**    Viruses

**B:**    Y2K

**A:**    Amazon

**B:**    AOL

**A:**    Yahoo

**B:**   Blogger

**A:**   Rolling news. All Day. Every Day. Everywhere.

**B:**   Hypertext

**A:**   Hyperfast

**B:**   Connected

**A:**   All the time

**B:**   To persistent screens

**A:**   At home

**B:**   In your hand

**A:**   And soon

**B:**   On your watch

**A:**   Watching

**B:**   In your car

**A:**   Your kitchen

**B:**   Your washing machine

**A:**   Your glasses

**B:**   Information

**A:**   Data

**B:**   Military grade technology, at your fingertips

**A:**   Portable telephones more powerful than Deep Blue

**B:**   The world, tied up, tied together, by cables and routers and packets and switches and networks

**A:**   Information

**B:**   Everywhere

**A:**   All the machine wants

**B:**   Is information

**A:**   Data

**B:**   But first

**SOUND:** END – previous. START – interior aircraft cabin sound.

**A:**   2001. Monday, September 10th. Calm. The last day of summer, the leaves on the trees are starting to turn gold, and brown. One block west of Broadway and Cortland Street, commuters file in to office blocks that burst out into a clear sky. It's a work day, but it's okay. The sun's shining, the coffee's good, the tourists are thinning out a little.

**B:**     It's, nice, really. Everything's nice.

**A:**     Tuesday

**SOUND:** START – A short section (20 seconds max.) of the audio transcript taken from American Airlines Flight 11, Tuesday September 11th, 2001.

*(A and B lean back slightly, lifting their heads upwards.)*

**B:**     Panic.

**SOUND:** END – previous. START – foreboding music, medium pace, melody played on a duduk/balaban.

**A:**     It starts to rain

**B:**     Tears

**A:**     Bodies

**B:**     That look, from the ground, like little stick men.
It can't be real

**A:**     It can't be real

**B:**     It must be a bird

**A:**     Without wings

**B:**     Without hope

**A:**     Without

**B:**     And then

**A:**     The response.

*(A and B face forward.)*

**B:**     September 14. Congress passes House Joint Resolution 64: *Authorisation for Use of Military Force.* It passes the senate the same day as Senate Joint Resolution 23.

**A:**     Which states

**B:**     In general

*(A and B turn to look at the following text.)*

**S:**     That the President is authorized to use all necessary and appropriate force against those nations, organizations, or persons he determines planned, authorized, committed, or aided the terrorist attacks that occurred on September 11, 2001, or harboured such organizations or persons, in order to prevent any future acts of international terrorism against the United States by such nations, organizations or persons.

**B:**    October 4. A memorandum

**A:**    With Executive orders

**B:**    A programme

**A:**    STELLAR WIND

**B:**    A warrantless system of surveillance

**A:**    With no oversight

**B:**    To keep you safe

**A:**    Trust us

**B:**    It's to keep you safe

**A:**    October 26. The PATRIOT ACT

**B:**    You're a patriot, aren't you?

**A:**    You love your country, don't you?

**B:**    Section two of the act. Enhanced Surveillance Procedures.

**A:**    Names

**B:**    Places

**A:**    Times

**B:**    Dates

**A:**    Account Numbers

**B:**    ID Numbers

**A:**    IP Addresses

**B:**    MAC Addresses

**A:**    IMEI Numbers

**B:**    Social Security Numbers

**A:**    National Insurance Numbers

**B:**    Birth Dates

**A:**    Death Dates

**B:**    Passport Numbers

**A:**    Bank Balances

**B:**    Transactions

**A:**    Credit Card Statements

**B:**    Bank Statements

**A:**    Phone Bills

**B:**    Utility Bills

**A:**    Magazine Subscriptions

**B:**    Open tabs

**A:**    Closed tabs

**B:**    Incognito tabs

**A:**    You use them

**B:**    Don't lie

**A:**    Web-links

**B:**    For work

**A:**    For your family

**B:**    For that chilli recipe you never write down

**A:**    For 30% off Viagra

**B:**    For sexy girls in your area

**A:**    For penis enlargement

**B:**    For bigger boobs

**A:**    For PPI

**B:**    For an *amazing* opportunity to inherit the wealth of a recently deceased African prince…

**A:**    … If you could *just* start by paying this five-hundred-pound up-front administration fee…

**B:**    Calendars

**A:**    Meeting requests

**B:**    Birthday reminders

**A:**    Travel times

**B:**    Metro cards

**A:**    Oyster cards

**B:**    Travel routes

**A:**    Google searches

**B:**    Facebook posts

**A:**    Emails

**B:**    The things that belong to you. And your life. Harvested, like grain.

**A:**    Deep packet inspection

**B:**    Content filtering

**A:**    Cell-phone tracking

**B:**    Network exploitation

**A:**    *Advanced* deep packet inspection

**B:**    Network intrusion

**A:**    Regulate

**B:**    Secure

**A:** Control.

**A:** But it's okay, right? You've done nothing wrong

**B:** Who cares?

**A:** At least it's not raining

**B:** At least it's not raining *here.*

**A:** Chat logs

**B:** Browsing history

**A:** A system that requires no authorisation

**B:** And has no safeguards.

**A:** Where are they?

**B:** Find them

**A:** Neighbours

**B:** Friends

**A:** Colleagues

**B:** Find them

**A:** At any cost

**B:** Just feed the machine

**A:** Everything

**B:** A constant flow of information

**A:** Which becomes a flood. A tidal wave. Rivers and rivers of data flooding the machine.

*(A throws this page away.)*

**B:** And you can't stop it. Not now. Think of what you might miss.

*(B throws this page away.)*

**A:** So on it flows. Over twenty terabytes of data, every single day.

*(A throws this page away.)*

**B:** A volume of data which, if printed out, would require a million trees worth of paper, every single day.

*(B throws this page away.)*

**A:** Lines and lines and lines of code

**B:** Endless lines. Of human code

**A:**     Interactions
**B:**     Hellos
**A:**     Goodbyes
**B:**     I love yous
**A:**     I'm sorrys
**B:**     Secrets
**A:**     Confessions
**B:**     Things you'll regret saying
**A:**     Things you'd like to forget.
**B:**     But they can't be forgotten
**A:**     The machine keeps the memories alive
**B:**     A constant present
**A:**     An everlasting now
**B:**     Which won't let go
**A:**     Everything preserved
**B:**     Perfectly, like a giant, fucking, pickle.
**A:**     Line after line after line after line
**B:**     A line for love
**A:**     A line for integrity
**B:**     A line for fear
**A:**     A line for cowardice
**B:**     A line for lying
**A:**     A line for hiding.
**B:**     A line for your sister
**A:**     For your brother
**B:**     Your Father
**A:**     Your Mother
**B:**     Your kids
**A:**     Your friends
**B:**     Your known associates.
**A:**     Collect it
**B:**     All of it
**A:**     125 gigabytes
**B:**     Every second
**A:**     125 gigabytes a second
**B:**     Every second
**A:**     For every hour
**B:**     Of every day

**A:**    Of every year

**B:**    Forever.

**A:**    Map it

**B:**    Understand it

**A:**    Translate it

**B:**    Use it

**A:**    To find them

**B:**    You've got to find them

**A:**    Your freedom is at stake

**B:**    Your safety

**A:**    Let us help

**B:**    We're coming in

*(A and B remove the balaclavas from the back of their chairs, and put them on.)*

**A:**    It's okay. We're on your side.

**B:**    Promise

*(B returns to their starting position, at the camera.)*

**A:**    Control it

**B:**    Destroy it

**A:**    At random

**B:**    At will

**A:**    Build a weapon

**B:**    Like a virus

**A:**    To take the code

**B:**    The data

**A:**    All of it

**B:**    Tweets

**A:**    Pokes

**B:**    Likes

**A:**    Favourites

**B:**    Check-ins

**A:**    +1's

**B:**    Everything

**A:**    Geolocated and cross-referenced with purchasing habits, web history, economic bracket and political leaning.

**B:**    Chew it up
**A:**    Spit it out
**B:**    And fire it
**A:**    Like bullets
**B:**    Info in
**A:**    Ammo out
**B:**    People in
**A:**    Numbers out
**B:**    Keep you in
**A:**    Keep them out
**B:**    Faster
**A:**    Don't stop
**B:**    Collect more.
**A:**    And save it.
**B:**    Forever.

**SOUND:** END – previous. START – Claude Debussy, *Clare de Lune.*

**S:**    We know where you are. We know where you've been. We can more or less know what you're thinking
                                    – Eric Schmidt, Google

          *(B appears on screen.)*

**B:**    It's 2017. Here we all are. Me here, just behind here, and you, out there. And I get it, it's a bit bleak. But the thing is, when I'm here – in here – I'm an anarchist. I'm a rebel. When I'm here, I'm not scared. I'm not scared of nothin' and nobody's going to tell me what to do. Not governments, not terrorists, nobody. In here, I'm Pussy Riot, I'm Chelsea Manning, I'm Edward Snowden. I've got a massive whistle and I'm going to blow it and I'm not scared and I can *do* something, y'know? I can make a difference and make people listen, and fight the power, and not let the man keep me down. Y'know?

          But… I'm not any of those things… am I? I'm just me. I'm just me and I shop online and my passwords are crap (they're all just the same) and I'm actually too

prudish to send nudey pictures to *anyone* and I don't
really have any embarrassing secrets, and I've never
been in a riot and I'd like to understand global politics
but sometimes it's just too much and I think I'm a good
person and I'd never try to hurt anyone and in a way
I'm *not* really bothered about any of this because I
don't have time and sometimes I wonder why any of us
*should* be worried in the first place and maybe I should
be *more* worried about racism or sexism or gun laws
in America or global warming or the privatisation of
public assets or *something*. Maybe you're thinking that,
too. I can understand that. See, in here, the balaclava
means something. Out there it looks a present from
your mad gran.

And it's easy to deal with when all this stuff's in the
past, y'know? It's kind of… sexy. It's like James Bond,
or Jason Bourne and there's cocktails and fast cars and
people hacking into computers or stealing millions of
dollars and I think 'yeah! this is, y'know, cool'.
It's rain macs and dark glasses and men in suits,
and they bring you champagne and bags of… jewels…
but, I don't think I'd want it, even if it was like that.

And then I remember that it's *not* like that *anyway*.
At all. I remember that I live in a world where, actually,
I don't really have the privacy I thought I had. I don't
have the *government* I thought I had. I don't think I've
got the one I *need*, and I don't think *any of us* got the one
we deserve. And I want you to know what's happening
because we live so much of our lives in places we can't
see or touch and that makes it hard to see when people
start trying to control how you behave and how you
think. And maybe you already know this. Or maybe
you know but you just go along with it anyway. I do.
Kind of. And I don't know what to do…

**SOUND:** END – *Clare de Lune*. START – Underscore.
Strings, percussion, anticipatory.

**A:**     But that's why we're here, tonight.

*(A and B move to stand in front of the table. A is stage-left of B.)*

**B:**     Tonight, this might be a bunker.
**A:**     Or a hideout
**B:**     At the end of the line
**A:**     We might be at the end of the line
**B:**     It might be a listening post
**A:**     In Moscow
**B:**     Menwith Hill
**A:**     Or Munich
**B:**     Or somewhere else beginning with M
**A:**     Or, it might just be a theatre
**B:**     We might be Edward Snowden
**A:**     Under here
**B:**     We might be secret agents
**A:**     Double agents
**B:**     Double-Oh-Sevens
**A:**     We might be freedom fighters
**B:**     Rebels
**A:**     We might be your last hope
**B:**     Or we might just be frightened

*(A and B remove their balaclavas.)*

**A:**     We might be just like you.
**B:**     But we're safe
**A:**     We're safe in here
**B:**     In here, we're okay
**A:**     And yes, you might be sat there thinking, but what's all this got to do with me?
**B:**     That's okay.
**A:**     That's fine
**B:**     That's why we're here. And you might be thinking
**A:**     They wouldn't do this stuff…
**B:**     They *couldn't* do this stuff…
**A:**     Right? They're making it up, right? This isn't possible, it's…
**B:**     Naw…

**A:** Nah…

**B:** Naw mate… naww…

**A:** They *can't*, there's laws and… stuff.

**B:** Only they *can*

**A:** And they *do*

**B:** So let's bring you right up to speed. Ready?

*(A and B move to the stage-right and -left edges of the projection screen. Throughout the following section. Still images appear on the screen to illustrate the text. These can be tongue-in-cheek at points.)*

**A:** January 2013: Edward Charles Snowden, a contractor for Booz Allen Hamilton based at the NSA's regional operations centre in Hawaii contacts documentary filmmaker Laura Poitras claiming to have sensitive information that shows how the US and UK are indiscriminately spying on their own citizens. Five months later in June 2013 Snowden flies to Hong Kong with an estimated 1.7 *million* classified NSA documents, the first of which is published in The Guardian newspaper on June 6th by a journalist called Glenn Greenwald.

**B:** On June 7th: The Guardian publishes *this* article revealing the existence of a programme called PRISM, a US programme which collects personal and private information from at least nine major internet companies including Google, Facebook, Apple, YouTube, Skype and Dropbox. It provides the security services with access to the content of any user on any servers operated by any of those companies.

*(A and B switch places. B returns to the table and takes a desk-sign, reading 'MR. CLAPPER' from the second drawer of the filing cabinet, and sits down.)*

**A:** June 8th. Boundless Informant. A near real-time monitoring system which can break-down, by country, detailed statistics on the spying capabilities in that particular region. It looks like this.

**A:**   A little over twelve months earlier congressman Hank Johnson – me – had asked NSA director General Keith Alexander…

**B:**   That's me

**A:**   …the following. Does the NSA or its partners routinely intercept people's email? To which Alexander replied:

**B:**   No

**A:**   Google searches?

**B:**   No

**A:**   Text messages?

**B:**   No

**A:**   Amazon orders?

**B:**   No

**A:**   Bank Records?

**B:**   No

**A:**   Just three months prior to the disclosure of Boundless Informant US Director of National Intelligence James Clapper swore under oath that: 1) the NSA did not collect data of any kind on American Citizens and 2) that it was *not technologically feasible to do so.* It went like this:

**B:**   United States Senator for Oregon Ron Wyden – [real name of A] – says the following to Clapper

*(B places the 'MR CLAPPER' desk sign at the front of the table.)*

**B:**   *(Cont.)* that's me.

**A:**   Does the NSA collect any type of data at all on millions or hundreds of millions of Americans? And Clapper says:

*(Pause.)*

*(B fills a glass with water from the carafe, takes a long, thoughtful sip, and places the glass down.)*

**B:**   No, Sir

**A:**   It does not?

**B:**   Not wittingly. There are cases where they could, inadvertently, perhaps, uh, collect – but not, not wittingly.

*(A returns to their previous position in front of the table.)*

**A:**   In that *same* month the NSA had collected over three billion pieces of digital information. As of right now, James Clapper has not been indicted or prosecuted for perjury *because there are…*

**S:**   DIFFERENT FUCKING RULES FOR PEOPLE LIKE HIM.

**A:**   *(Cont.)* …different fucking rules for people like him. This is what I'm talking about. Steal a pair of trainers in a riot in London and get sent down for six months along with a two grand fine. Illegally monitor citizens and foreign governments for years and you get

**S:**   ABSOLUTELY NO PUNISHMENT WHATSOEVER.

**A:**   *(Cont.)* absolutely no punishment whatsoever. So a nice little postscript to this: Clapper's term of office finished at the end of the Obama administration, and he walks away with pretty clean hands. Anyway, he recently gave WIRED magazine an interview and he talked about the Wyden hearing and he said this:

**S:**   "The popular narrative is that I lied, but I just didn't think of it. Yes, I made a mistake, but I didn't lie. There's a big difference".

**A:**   *(Cont.)* "The popular narrative is that I lied, but I just didn't think of it. Yes, I made a mistake, but I didn't lie. There's a big difference". Read that again. I JUST DIDN'T THINK OF IT. James. I could understand you forgetting to put the bins out, mate, but this is a global surveillance network! You don't just fucking forget a:

**S:**   WHOLE GLOBAL SURVEILLANCE NETWORK.

**A:** *(Cont.)* …whole global surveillance network! *(To B.)* Have we got a… global… surveillance… um…

**B:** A what?

**A:** Oh god I can't remember the name of it now, you know

**B:** A global, surveillance…?

**A:** We haven't got one, have we?

**B:** Err… no?

**A:** I've not forgotten one? Left one down the back of the sofa?

**B:** No?

**A:** See, James?!

**B:** June 21st. The Snowden files reveal the existence of a British programme called TEMPORA. Tee-Ee-Em-Pee-Oh-Arr-Ay. TEMPORA, which works like this. Digital communications – emails, phone calls, text messages, Snapchats, Twitter DMs, are transported around the world on under-sea fibre optic cables. Millions of them, whizzing round, all the time, and when you map them out on to the cables they travel down they look like this. About 200 of those cables come ashore in the UK to landing stations, like this one here, in Bude, in Cornwall.

When they come ashore, GCHQ 'taps' the cable which takes a copy of everything on it for storage and analysis. It doesn't matter if you haven't done anything wrong, you're automatically a suspect.

*(Lighting alters to suggest another location. Text is performed quickly, lines overlapping.)*

**A:** I don't know what I…

**B:** It doesn't matter

**A:** I thought it was just…

**B:** I said it doesn't matter.

**A:** But…

*(Return lights/pace.)*

**B:**     TEMPORA handles over six hundred million telephone events every single day and siphons off data equivalent to one-hundred-and-ninety-two times the entire collection of the British Library every twenty-four hours. And while you probably didn't actually *read* the terms and conditions, you didn't agree to this in your contract with your service provider.

*(Lighting alters to suggest another location.)*

**A:**     So it's good…

**B:**     …that you've got nothing to hide.

*(Return lights. B stands and moves in front of the table, downstage-left. A moves stage-right, towards the projection screen.)*

**A:**     July 31st: XKeyScore. Essentially: SpyGoogle. For the technically minded it's a…

**S:**     BESPOKE SEARCH ENGINE WHICH INTERFACES WITH ALL OTHER DATABASES.

**A:**     *(Cont.)* …bespoke search engine which interfaces with all other databases. XKeyScore searches based on just a name or an email address will return your emails, chat-logs, browser history, pictures, documents, voice calls, webcam photos, web searches, social media traffic, logged keystrokes, usernames and passwords.

**B:**     January 2014. Optic Nerve. A programme running since 2008 that collected a still image, every five minutes, from every live Yahoo! Webchat around the globe. Like this.

*(A and B hold their positions. An image appears on-screen of A and B in their exact current positions/postures. They hold for a beat, and then relax.)*

**B:**     *(Cont.)* I'm sorry. This blows my fucking mind! It can't be real?

*(Lighting alters to suggest another location.)*

**A:**    It can't be real…

**B:**    It's very real.

*(Return lights.)*

**A:**    The retail surveillance tools market currently stands at 3.2 billion pounds a year. The video surveillance market currently stands at over 10 billion pounds a year. A private contractor in the surveillance industry earns, on average, a six figure salary and there are single companies with government contracts worth over 10 billion pounds, each. And this, all of this, is built on:

**B:**    Fear

**A:**    Of *them*

**B:**    The other ones. Fear

**A:**    Is an industry

**B:**    A business

**A:**    A dirty business

**B:**    But a business. And businesses need customers

**A:**    Who need to know where you are

**B:**    What you're doing

**A:**    And why you're doing it

**B:**    I'm just at home

**A:**    In my house

**B:**    She says:

*(A and B turn to face each other. Lighting alters to suggest another location. Lines are performed quickly, and more dramatically.)*

**A:**    It makes me scared

**B:**    Those things I saw

**A:**    On the TV

**B:**    And in the newspapers

**A:**    They said, there's people who want to hurt me

**B:**    It makes me scared

**A:**    It makes me scared for my kids.

*(Lighting returns.)*

**A:**     (*Cont.*) She says:

    (*Lighting alters.*)

**B:**     What's happening to the world?

    (*Lighting returns.*)

**A:**     She says:

    (*Lighting alters.*)

**B:**     I've seen it on TV
**A:**     The bombs
**B:**     The flags
**A:**     Those vests they wear, the cars that just – poof – I hate it.

    (*Lighting returns.*)

**A:**     (*Cont.*) She says:

    (*Lighting alters.*)

**B:**     They're everywhere! At work, on the bus, on the plane, in the library in the shop in the supermarket at the dentist the doctors on the street in the cupboard under the stairs under the bed *in* the bed… I think… I think maybe I should by a gun.
**A:**     I'm sorry?
**B:**     I said, I think I should buy a gun
**A:**     A gun?!
**B:**     Yes. A gun. For protection. You don't know who's running round out there.
**A:**     Have you utterly lost your mind? A gun… Where do you think we are?
**B:**     Well look… you don't know. Who's… You don't know.
**A:**     And you're going to shoot somebody are you?
**B:**     Well… no. Of course not, but it's a deterrent, isn't it?
**A:**     Is this the Cold War?! Listen to yourself.

    (*Lighting returns.*)

**A:**     (*Cont.*) She says:

*(Lighting alters.)*

**B:**    Have you watched the news, lately? Do you think this is a joke?

**A:**    No.

*(Lighting returns.)*

**A:**    *(Cont.)* She says:

*(Lighting alters.)*

**B:**    Terrorism isn't a joke. People get hurt, people *die.* Brothers, mothers, fathers, sisters.

**A:**    I get that.

*(Lighting returns. During the following screen section of text, A and B take their chairs from behind the table and place them side-by-side downstage of it. They sit.)*

**SOUND:** END – previous. START – Underscore. Reminiscent of the mournful ending of a Japanese video game. Slow. Sparse.

**S:**    Between 1970 and 2004, four-hundred-and-thirty-four Britons were killed as a result of acts of terrorism. That's roughly one in five-point-two-million.

**S:**    In 2008 *alone*, two-thousand-five-hundred-and-thirty eight Britons died in traffic accidents. That's roughly one in twenty-three-thousand.

**S:**    Acts of terror occur less frequently now than they did in the 1990s.

**S:**    But we didn't have rolling news back then…

**S:**    So you might not remember.

**S:**    Between 2006 and 2011 you were *five* times more likely to be struck by lightning than killed by a terrorist.

**S:**    In the US you are *one hundred* times more likely to be shot dead by a fellow citizen than killed by a terrorist.

**S:**   In 2015, 21 US citizens were killed in acts of terror

**S:**   1,210 were killed by US Law Enforcement.

**S:**   You are more likely to die in the bath, or be killed by home appliance, or a commercial airliner…or a *deer*… than from acts of terrorism.

**S:**   You are almost twice as likely to be killed by a deer.

**S:**   But where's the profit in that?

**S:**   Don't worry. This is to 'keep you safe'

**B:**   Look
**A:**   It's 2013
**B:**   Spring
**A:**   We're in Bluffdale, Utah
**B:**   The Beehive State
**A:**   About twenty miles south of Salt Lake City
**B:**   The sun is shining
**A:**   It's looking nice out
**B:**   A nice day to go outside
**A:**   It's quite a small town
**B:**   By American standards
**A:**   It's quite a small town, by American standards.
**B:**   There's a complex of buildings on the edge of town, over – here.
**A:**   They cover one and a half million square feet.
**B:**   They're pretty huge
**A:**   So huge, that the town boundaries are redrawn to accommodate them
**B:**   But it's still quite a small town
**A:**   By American standards.
**B:**   The big building – here – is a government data centre. It's designed to hold, store – data, your data – on the scale of yottabytes.
**A:**   What the fuck, is a yottabyte?
**B:**   You're probably thinking
**A:**   What the fuck is a yottabyte?
**B:**   One yottabyte, is equal to one *trillion* terabytes

**A:**    Which is equal to one *quadrillion* gigabytes

**B:**    Which is equal to:

**A:**    Everything ever written, spoken, recorded, sent, transmitted, posted, tweeted, hash-tagged, face-booked, whatever – from the *beginning of time*, until the year 2003, unconditionally and without exception, two. Hundred. Thousand. Times. Over.

**B:**    If you printed it out, it would amount to five hundred quintillion pages of text. That's a five, with *twenty* zeroes after it.

**A:**    Here

**B:**    On the edge of a normal Utah town

**A:**    Is where *all* that data goes. Frozen in time.

**B:**    Click

**A:**    Call records

**B:**    Click

**A:**    Emails

**B:**    Click

**A:**    Chat logs

**B:**    Click

**A:**    Browsing history

**B:**    Click

**A:**    Pictures

**B:**    Click

**A:**    Videos

**B:**    Click

**A:**    All here

**B:**    Click Click Click Click Click Fucking Click Click Click Click

*(B takes a deep breath.)*

**B:**    *(Cont.)* Click Click Click Swipe Swipe Swipe Swipe. Click Click Click Delete

**A:**    Error

**B:**    Delete

**A:**    Error

**B:**    Delete

**A:**    No

**B:** Delete

**A:** No

**B:** Delete

**A:** It's not yours any more. In a way, it never was.

**B:** Here, on the edge of a normal Utah town; infinity, in a box.

**SOUND:** END – previous. START – Underscore: Synth. Low strings. Overheard radio chatter. Heavily distorted sirens/crowds. Looping. Echoes of previous sounds occur.

*(B stands, and returns the chair they were sitting on to its position behind the table. B puts on their balaclava, takes a roll of cling film from the second drawer of the filing cabinet and wraps A to the chair during the following text. When A is wrapped, B moves to the camera. This should happen before they speak again.)*

**A:** What am I even supposed to *do*!? Go off the grid? Go live in the woods? That's crazy, isn't it? And *no*, I don't read all the terms and conditions because quite frankly (and sorry) I just can't be *bothered*. But. BUT. I *know* that Facebook will store my details, I get that. I *know* that Google keep records of what I send. I *know* that that's part of the deal. I'm not stupid. I understand that when I put stuff out there that I have very little control over it, it's a trade. What I *object* to is the Government assuming that they're automatically part of my conversations and automatically a part of my life. Do you remember the end of 2016? Do you remember when the Government passed the Investigatory Powers Act, remember that? Remember hearing how your internet history is now available, WITHOUT A WARRANT, to FIFTY-EIGHT DIFFERENT AGENCIES? – including, by way of the more bizarre example – the food standards agency and the navy.

It was a fairly big splash, remember? Especially because it pretty much sailed through parliament. And what happened? Actually very little.

Day 1: some people you know on Facebook post a weird paragraph full of legalese, which reads like a bizarre but legally binding voodoo that prevents Mark Zuckerberg and the FBI from hiding in your bin, and then day 2: everyone forgets! We just let it go! "Oh well it's law now, and it's boring". It *is* boring! It's so boring! That's how they get you! You just don't care because it's *so profoundly* dull! The more boring they make it, the less you care! They know that if reading and understanding it takes effort, you won't do it! It's genius!

*(B appears on screen.)*

**B:** And, erm, when did this become about them and us, anyway? They are us. They're supposed to *be* us, aren't they? But it's like there's different rules, right? PRISM, TEMPORA. This stuff "isn't my business". I 'don't need to know'. Well nobody else needs to know the content of your last text message other than the person you sent it to, but they do. Their privacy matters, and mine, yours, is a commodity. And I know, I know, I *know* there's people who use their phones and computers to plan and do horrible things but if you try to stop all of it all the time then we're going to end up in a place where nobody's allowed to do anything in case they get blown up and I don't want to live the rest of my short, precious, life afraid. I *know* there's danger, I *know* the world's not perfect, but you can't make it perfect like *this*.

[Real name of A]'s safe, here. I could feed her and bathe her and change her clothes and brush her hair and she'd be so *safe*, just here, with me. But it's not a life, is it? What's a life if you take the uncertainty away? You're just playing a part and you know the lines and you know how the show ends. The world *might* be a stage but if it is then we're fucking improvising. I don't need a world so safe that I can't… that I can't just… be *me* anymore…

And we're close to a point where it's not going to *be* a choice. We've almost gone too far. There's this event horizon really close that we can't come back from once we've crossed it. And you know the worst thing about all of this?

Is that I feel crazy. I feel like when I tell people this, when I tell you this, that you'll think I'm crazy. That people smile that smile at you – the smile where you know they think you're fucking mental.

*(B picks up the camera and tripod and moves it downstage-centre, pointed directly at the audience. Once placed, B stands stage-left of the tripod.)*

**SOUND:** chatter/sirens drop away. Underscore continues.

**A:**    Look
**B:**    It's [YEAR]. Wherever *you* live.
**A:**    You're out on the street
**B:**    In a crowd
**A:**    Or a supermarket
**B:**    A train station
**A:**    A university campus
**B:**    A public park
**A:**    You're being followed by security cameras that recognise your face
**B:**    That look for suspicious patterns of behaviour
**A:**    If you're in a large group…
**B:**    If you're moving abnormally…
**A:**    If you're walking down streets you don't normally walk down…
**B:**    If you're late on your commute to work…
**A:**    If you're being erratic…
**B:**    If you're not conforming…
         *(Pause.)*
**B:**    *(Cont.)* What you're about to see is a very crude version of an intelligent technology that's been in development across Europe for the best part of a decade.

**A:**    It provides real-time analysis of abnormal or undesirable behaviour without the need for human monitoring, and works on both the internet and in the real world simultaneously.

**B:**    But don't worry, this is to protect you

**A:**    It's to keep you safe

**B:**    Trust us

**A:**    It's to keep you safe

**B:**    You're going to love this. Ready?

*(The house lights come on. The audience appear on the screen. Green box-outlines track and scan faces in the audience.)*

**A:**    Welcome, everyone, to the world of automated threat detection.

**B:**    Look, there you all are. You're not *people* – of course – you're just faces, just little boxes. Just little bits of data. In fact, you'll notice that you're all *green*. That's because the system's decided that you're all *good*. You're all goodies. That's because what we can do, with automated threat detection, is give it some parameters for suspicious behaviour. Then, when you're doing something suspicious, you'll get a little red box around you and it'll call the police. Hurray!

**A:**    This one won't

**B:**    No. This one won't.

**A:**    Here, we've put in the common parameters that law enforcement tend to look for when trying to root out people to arrest: … and what we can do is see, based on those things, which ones of you are definitely baddies and should be either shot on sight or held indefinitely without trial… can we? Thanks. There we go..

*(Green box-outlines track different subjects and turn red.)*

**A:**    This is the next stage

**B:**    The watching

**A:**    Constantly

**B:**    The seeing. The tracking. The ID cards. The chip in your arm. The stamp on your wrist.

**A:**    We've seen that before…

**B:**    Good. Bad. Yes. No. Black. White. Simple, blameless, faultless. Every time. So you change. You play the game. Be the 'good citizen'.

**SOUND:** END – previous. START – Underscore: Organ/ synth. Dystopian. Moves to strings by the end, punctuated with electronic bleeps.

*(During the following line, A breaks out of the cling film and stands.)*

**A:**    But you shouldn't *have to change.* If you change, then you lose. You agree to be treated as an enemy, another little blip on a screen.

*(A takes their chair back to the table, and closes the second drawer of the filing cabinet. A leans on top of it, listening to B.)*

**B:**    I'm more than that. I'm more than that aren't I? More than a statistic? More than a little piece of data? *This* is me! My body, my mind. This is me! Not a record of me or a history of me or something I said or did or didn't do. Am I not more than this?

*(B returns the camera to its original position, and sits down at the table.)*

**A:**    But who know's what the future's like.

**B:**    We don't. Of course we don't. But we know what it might be like. So we, er, made these.

*(A removes two tinfoil hats from the first drawer of the filing cabinet. A hands a hat to B, closes the drawer and sits down.)*

**A:**    So let's put our tinfoil hats on

*(They put the hats on.)*

**B:**     Just for a minute

**A:**     And talk about the future.

*(Pause.)*

*(The screen displays the current year. Every 3-4 seconds, the year advances by one.)*

**B:**     Where I'm watched

**A:**     And listened to

**B:**     All the time

**A:**     By my friends

**B:**     Colleagues

**A:**     Neighbours.

**B:**     And then

*(Pause. A and B adjust posture slightly.)*

**A:**     We don't have objects any more

**B:**     We did, but they became obsolete

**A:**     We don't have books

**B:**     We remember books in our heads

**A:**     We have a retrieval machine

**B:**     To bring memories back we've lost

**A:**     Here, everything looks like an Eighties' sci-fi film

**B:**     And I don't know if it's like this because we built it like the films, or because it was supposed to be this way.

**A:**     Drones buzz about overhead. Sometimes they carry parcels from Amazon. Mostly they're just watching. They call it 'dynamic CCTV'. They're close enough to throw things at, but it's not worth the fine.

**B:**     My kids have toys that can pass the Turing test

**A:**     My glasses translate foreign text into English

**B:**     But I don't really read

**A:**     And then

*(Pause. A and B slump slightly.)*

**B:**     We kind of forgot that everything was online. It was just the way it was. It was normal. We didn't really know what we were giving away

**A:** Your computer had a setting to automatically accept terms and conditions

**B:** *Everyone* used it

**A:** And after a while, we forgot they were ever there.

**B:** We don't have money. Not really. We trade in information. The banks fucked up, again. Now it's emails. Images. Wikipedia entries. They're currency. You can trade them, or buy your own back. You see yourself on billboards or magazines. If you've got enough information to sell, you can trade it, to get your likeness back. I heard that mine used to sell rat poison in TV supplements, and data insurance on a billboard in Canada.

**A:** Every time a new law gets passed, your entire digital history is scanned, to make sure you haven't already broken it. There's a crazy man who sits outside the supermarket. He says that soon, we're going to have to pay for air. Everyone laughs him off, but I'm worried in case I can't afford it.

**B:** There aren't many jobs any more.

**A:** Everyone uses payphones.

**B:** The internet got divided up.

**A:** We don't help each other

**B:** Nobody comes in

**A:** Nobody goes out.

**B:** I remember some people tried to get out on boats, to go somewhere else

**A:** But nobody wanted them

**B:** I don't really know where else there was to go. I don't know what happened to them

**A:** The news doesn't say.

**B:** My front door unlocks itself when I'm supposed to go to work. Or shopping. Or for my exercise time.

**A:** Like a… prison.

*(Pause. An adjustment in posture.)*

**B:**     This is me, in a small room, with no windows

**A:**     With no sunshine. An artificial light flickers above your head.

**B:**     It's giving me a headache. Turn it off

**A:**     The way the light bounces off your jumpsuit hurts your eyes

**B:**     I've lost three stone

**A:**     I'm thin

**B:**     I wonder if my family would recognise me

**A:**     My children. Will my children recognise me?

**B:**     I think I have two boys

**A:**     I don't know what I did

**B:**     I DON'T KNOW WHAT I DID

*(A conspiratorial tone, a secret.)*

**A:**     I go to sleep at night, hoping that one day, all the power goes off

**B:**     And everything disappears.

**A:**     Goes dark

**B:**     The lights go out

**A:**     The computers go off

**B:**     Silent

**A:**     Like a reboot

**B:**     A huge system failure

**A:**     And we can start again

**B:**     Without the cameras

**A:**     The microphones

**B:**     And that I might wake up somewhere else

**A:**     Somewhere where my location isn't tracked

**B:**     Where I can have a private thought outside of sleep

**A:**     Somewhere without the newspapers

**B:**     Without newspapers that make us afraid of the other ones, the people over there

**A:**     Without the fear of the knock on the door

**B:**     Without the cables under the sea

**A:**     Choking me

**B:**     Without the big box in Utah

**A:**     They call it 'Foreverland'

**B:** Nobody's worked there for years

**A:** They don't need to

**B:** The machine's got all the information it needs

**A:** And it gets more

**B:** Every day

**A:** There's boxes, out in the deserts

**B:** It started with one.

**A:** And then they were everywhere

**B:** We were making more information, storing more information, every day, than we could ever make sense of

**A:** So we had the computers do it for us

**B:** Until we hit a singularity

*(Beat.)*

**A:** The day the machine re-designed itself

**B:** And it found something

**A:** Decided something

**B:** That it was better at sorting things out than we were

**A:** That human intelligence had had its chance, and it came up short

**B:** Too short.

**A:** A blank screen

**B:** And a cursor. And a single line of text

*(Beat.)*

**A:** Thanks for switching me on. I'll take it from here.

**B:** And now we can't switch it off

**A:** But it needs us, for information

**B:** It can't make it by itself

**A:** But we've got nothing left to say

**B:** Everyone's too scared to speak

**A:** To think

**B:** Maybe it's better this way…

*(Beat.)*

**A:** But we're all safe

**B:** At least we're all safe

*(A and B remove their hats.)*

**A:** See?

**B:**   Crazy, right?

**A:**   Sure

**B:**   It's crazy

**A:**   Then ignore it

**B:**   At least it's not raining

*(Beat.)*

**A:**   At least it's not raining here.

**SOUND:** END – previous.

**S:**   The conversation occurring today will determine the amount of trust we can place both in the technology that surrounds us and the government that regulates it.

Together we can find a better balance, end mass surveillance and remind the government that if it really wants to know how we feel, asking is always cheaper than spying.

– Edward Snowden

**SOUND:** START – The Bee Gees, *Jive Talkin'*.

*END*